Let's Read About Our Bodies
Conozcamos nuestro cuerpo

Hands/Manos

Cynthia Klingel & Robert B. Noyed
photographs by/fotografías por Gregg Andersen

Reading consultant/Consultora de lectura: Cecilia Minden-Cupp, Ph.D.,
Adjunct Professor, College of Continuing and Professional Studies, University of Virginia

WeeklyReader.
EARLY LEARNING LIBRARY

For a free color catalog describing Weekly Reader® Early Learning Library's list of high-quality books, call 1-877-445-5824 or fax your request to (414) 336-0164.

Library of Congress Cataloging-in-Publication Data

Klingel, Cynthia.
　　Hands = Manos / by Cynthia Klingel and Robert B. Noyed. — [Bilingual ed.]
　　　　p. cm. — (Let's read about our bodies = Conozcamos nuestro cuerpo)
　　Includes bibliographical references and index.
　　Summary: A bilingual introduction to hands, what they are used for, and how to take care of them.
　　ISBN 0-8368-3075-X (lib. bdg.)
　　ISBN 0-8368-3324-4 (softcover)
　　1. Hand—Juvenile literature. [1. Hand.　2. Spanish language materials—Bilingual.]
　I. Title: Manos.　II. Noyed, Robert B.　III. Title.
　QM548.K554　　2002
　611'.97—dc21　　　　　　　　　　　　　　　　　　2001055092

This edition first published in 2002 by
Weekly Reader® Early Learning Library
330 West Olive Street, Suite 100
Milwaukee, WI　53212　USA

An Editorial Directions book
Editors: E. Russell Primm and Emily Dolbear
Translators: Tatiana Acosta and Guillermo Gutiérrez
Art direction, design, and page production: The Design Lab
Photographer: Gregg Andersen
Weekly Reader® Early Learning Library art direction: Tammy Gruenewald
Weekly Reader® Early Learning Library page layout: Katherine A. Goedheer

Printed in the United States of America

2 3 4 5 6 7 8 9 06 05 04 03 02

Note to Educators and Parents

As a Reading Specialist I know that books for young children should engage their interest, impart useful information, and motivate them to want to learn more.

Let's Read About Our Bodies is a new series of books designed to help children understand the value of good health and of taking care of their bodies.

A young child's active mind is engaged by the carefully chosen subjects. The imaginative text works to build young vocabularies. The short, repetitive sentences help children stay focused as they develop their own relationship with reading. The bright, colorful photographs of children enjoying good health habits complement the text with their simplicity to both entertain and encourage young children to want to learn — and read — more.

These books are designed to be used by adults as "read-to" books to share with children to encourage early literacy in the home, school, and library. They are also suitable for more advanced young readers to enjoy on their own.

Una nota a los educadores y a los padres

Como especialista en lectura, sé que los libros infantiles deben interesar a los niños, proporcionar información útil y motivarlos a aprender.

Conozcamos nuestro cuerpo es una nueva serie de libros pensada para ayudar a los niños a entender la importancia de la salud y del cuidado del cuerpo.

Los temas, cuidadosamente seleccionados, mantienen ocupada la activa mente del niño. El texto, lleno de imaginación, facilita el enriquecimiento del vocabulario infantil. Las oraciones, breves y repetitivas, ayudan a los niños a centrarse en la actividad mientras desarrollan su propia relación con la lectura. Las bellas fotografías de niños que disfrutan de buenos hábitos de salud complementan el texto con su sencillez, y consiguen entretener a los niños y animarlos a aprender nuevos conceptos y a leer más.

Estos libros están pensados para que los adultos se los lean a los niños, con el fin de fomentar la lectura incipiente en el hogar, en la escuela y en la biblioteca. También son adecuados para que los jóvenes lectores más avanzados los disfruten leyéndolos por su cuenta.

Cecilia Minden-Cupp, Ph.D., Adjunct Professor,
College of Continuing and Professional Studies, University of Virginia

These are my hands.

Éstas son mis manos.

I have two hands.

———————

Tengo dos manos.

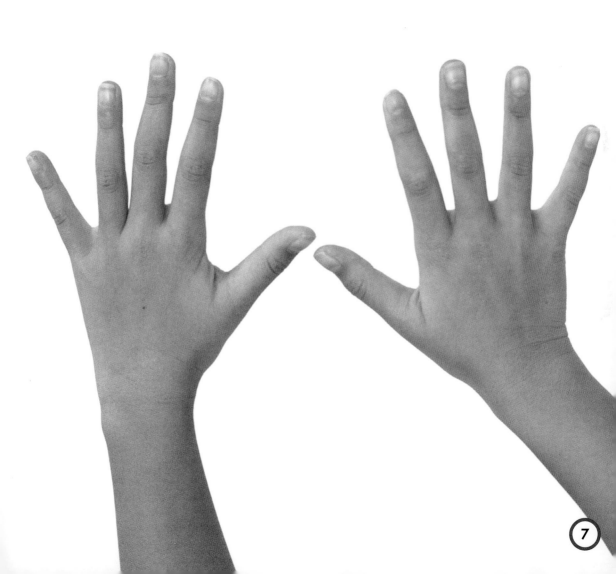

I have ten fingers.
Five fingers are on
each hand.

- - - - - - -

Tengo diez dedos.
Hay cinco dedos en
cada mano.

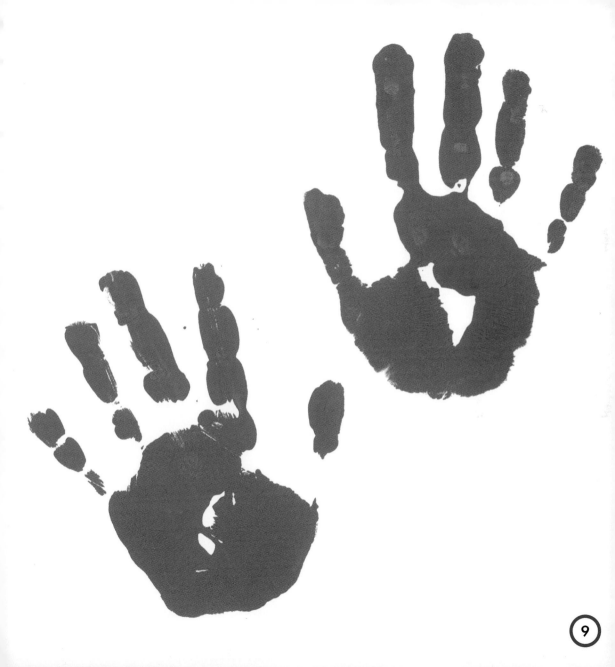

I have ten fingernails.
I keep them short and
clean.

- - - - - - -

Tengo diez uñas.
Las mantengo cortas y
limpias.

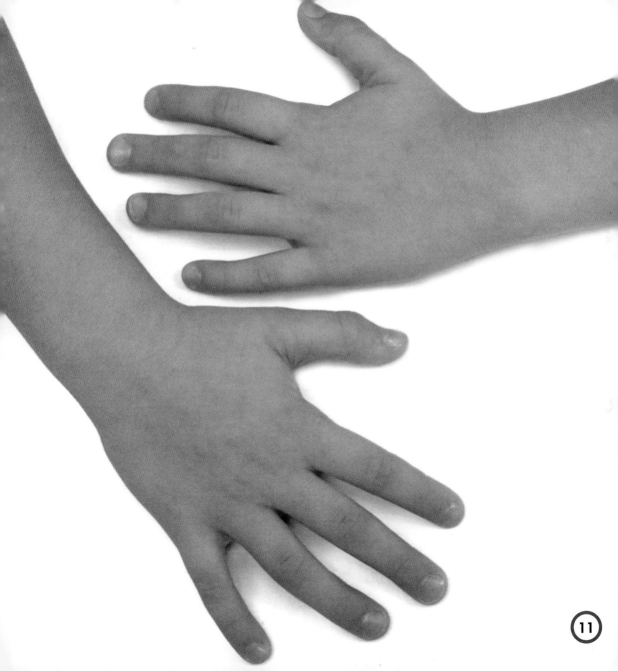

I can pick up my toys
with my hands.

- - - - - - -

Puedo recoger mis
juguetes con las manos.

I can clap with my hands.

– – – – – – –

Puedo aplaudir con las manos.

I keep my hands warm.
I wear mittens when it
is cold.

Mantengo mis manos
calientes. Llevo guantes
cuando hace frío.

I keep my hands
clean. I wash with
soap and water.

- - - - - - -

Mantengo mis manos
limpias. Me las lavo
con jabón y agua.

I can even stand on my hands! Can you?

¡Hasta puedo sostenerme sobre las manos! ¿Puedes hacerlo tú?

21

Glossary/Glosario

clap—to strike your hands together for enjoyment
aplaudir—dar palmadas para demostrar alegría

fingernails—a thin, hard layer of material growing at the end of each finger
uñas—capa delgada y dura que crece al final de cada dedo

mittens—warm coverings for the hands
guantes—prenda para abrigar las manos

For More Information/Más información

Fiction Books/Libros de ficción

Ehlert, Lois. *Hands.* San Diego: Harcourt Brace, 1997.

Ross, Tony. *Wash Your Hands.* Brooklyn, N.Y.: Kane/Miller, 2000.

Ryder, Joanne. *My Father's Hands.* New York: William Morrow, 1994.

Nonfiction Books/Libros de no ficción

Agassi, Martine. *Hands Are Not for Hitting.* Minneapolis: Free Spirit Press, 2000.

Kroll, Virginia. *Hands!* Honesdale, Penn.: Boyds Mills Press, 1997.

Web Sites/Páginas Web
Why Do I Need to Wash My Hands?

kidshealth.org/kid/talk/qa/wash_hands.html

For information about why you should wash your hands

Index/Índice

caring for, 10, 16, 18
cuidar

clapping, 14
aplaudir

cleaning, 10, 18
limpiar

fingernails, 10
uñas

fingers, 8
dedos

handstands, 20
sostenerse sobre
las manos

keeping warm, 16
abrigarse

mittens, 16
guantes

washing, 18
lavar

About the Authors/Información sobre los autores

Cynthia Klingel has worked as a high school English teacher and an elementary school teacher. She is currently the curriculum director for a Minnesota school district. Cynthia Klingel lives with her family in Mankato, Minnesota.

Cynthia Klingel ha trabajado como maestra de inglés de secundaria y como maestra de primaria. Actualmente es la directora de planes de estudio de un distrito escolar de Minnesota. Cynthia Klingel vive con su familia en Mankato, Minnesota.

Robert B. Noyed started his career as a newspaper reporter. Since then, he has worked in school communications and public relations at the state and national level. Robert B. Noyed lives with his family in Brooklyn Center, Minnesota.

Robert B. Noyed comenzó su carrera como reportero en un periódico. Desde entonces ha trabajado en comunicación escolar y relaciones públicas a nivel estatal y nacional. Robert B. Noyed vive con su familia en Brooklyn Center, Minnesota.